Team Work and Team Building

90 Minute Guides

Michelle N. Halsey

Silver City Publications & Training, L.L.C.
P.O. Box 1914
Nampa, ID 83653
https://www.silvercitypublications.com/shop/

ISBN-10: 1-64004-037-4
ISBN-13: 978-1-64004-037-3

Contents

Chapter 1 – Defining Success

For most of us, teamwork is a part of everyday life. Whether it's at home, in the community, or at work, we are often expected to be a functional part of a performing team. This workshop will encourage participants to explore the different aspects of a team, as well as ways that they can become a top-notch team performer.

By the end of this tutorial, you should be able to:

- Describe the concept of a team, and its factors for success

- Explain the four phases of the Tuckman team development model and define their characteristics

- List the three types of teams

- Describe actions to take as a leader – and as a follower for each of the four phases (Forming, Storming, Norming and Performing)

- Discuss the uses, benefits and disadvantages of various team-building activities

- Describe several team-building activities that you can use, and in what settings

- Follow strategies for setting and leading team meetings

- Detail problem-solving strategies using the Six Thinking Hats model -- and one consensus-building approach to solving team problems

- List actions to do -- and those to avoid -- when encouraging teamwork

Action Plans and Evaluation Forms

During this course, you will be adding ideas to your personal action plan. The plan uses the SMART system. This means that your goals must be **S**pecific, **M**easurable, **A**ttainable, **R**ealistic, and **T**imely.

Add information throughout the day as you learn new things and have ideas about how to incorporate the concepts being discussed into your work or personal lives.

Defining Success

Success is determined by a wide range of factors. When we are given a project or an assignment we are also usually given a metric to which we can gauge the success of it. Having a strong team will benefit any organization and will lead to more successes than not.

What is a Team?

A team is a group of people formed to achieve a goal. Teams can be temporary, or indefinite. With individuals sharing responsibility, the group as a whole can take advantage of all of the collective talent, knowledge, and experience of each team member.

Team building is an organized effort to improve team effectiveness.

An Overview of Tuckman and Jensen's Four-Phase Model

Educational psychologist Bruce Wayne Tuckman, Ph.D. was charged by his boss at the Naval Medical Research Institute, Bethesda MD with a review of 50 articles about team behavior. From this body of work, Dr. Tuckman conceived his theory of group developmental processes in 1965.

The Forming Stage: Groups initially concern themselves with orientation accomplished primarily through testing. Such testing serves to identify the boundaries of both interpersonal and task behaviors. Coincident with testing in the interpersonal realm is the establishment of dependency relationships with leaders, other group members, or preexisting standards. It may be said that orientation, testing, and dependence constitute the group process of forming.

The Storming Stage: The second point in the sequence is characterized by conflict and polarization around interpersonal issues, with concomitant emotional responding in the task sphere. These behaviors serve as resistance to group influence and task requirements and may be labeled as storming.

The Norming Stage: Resistance is overcome in the third stage in which in-group feeling and cohesiveness develop, new standards evolve, and new roles are adopted. In the task realm, intimate, personal opinions are expressed. Thus, we have the stage of norming.

The Performing Stage: Finally, the group attains the fourth and final stage in which interpersonal structure becomes the tool of task activities. Roles become flexible and functional, and group energy is channeled into the task. Structural issues have been resolved, and structure can now become supportive of task performance. This stage can be labeled as performing.

In 1977 Dr. Tuckman, collaborating with Mary Ann Jensen, proposed an update to the model, termed Adjourning. It describes the process for terminating group roles, task completion, and the reduction of dependencies. This stage has also been called "mourning", especially if the team's dissolution is unplanned. The first four stages are the most commonly used parts of the process.*

Smith, M. K. (2005) 'Bruce W. Tuckman - forming, storming, norming and performing in groups, the encyclopedia of informal education, www.infed.org/thinkers/tuckman.htm. © Mark K. Smith 2005

Chapter 2 – Types of Teams

The Merriam Webster Dictionary defines a team as a number of persons associated together in work or activity. Teams are formed for many purposes. Examples include project teams, ad-hoc teams, quality improvement teams, and task forces. Sometimes the team is formed to work on a goal as an adjunct to a traditional hierarchy in an organization. At other times, the team is designed to replace the hierarchy.

Several roles help to keep a team operating smoothly.

Role	Responsibilities
Team Leader	• Moves the team to accomplish its task • Provides a conducive environment for getting the work done (location, resources) • Communicates with the team
Team Facilitator	• Makes things happen with ease • Helps the group with the process • Enables the group to produce the "how" decisions Note: Facilitators may be members or non-members of the team.
Team Recorder	• Writes down the team's key points, ideas and decisions • Documents the team's process, discussions, and decisions
Time Keeper	• Monitors how long the team is taking to accomplish its tasks • Provides regular updates to the team on how well or poorly they are using their time • Collaborates with the team leader, facilitator and others to determine new time schedules if the agenda has to be adjusted

Team Members	• Displays enthusiasm and commitment to the team's purpose
	• Behaves honestly; maintain confidential information behind closed doors
	• Shares responsibility to rotate through other team roles
	• Shares knowledge and expertise and not withhold information
	• Asks questions
	• Respects the opinions and positions of others on the team, even if the person has an opposing view or different opinion

The Traditional Team

There are several characteristics common to traditional teams.

* A team gains a shared understanding and purpose among team members, as distinguished from a group.

* Teams require mutually agreed-upon operating principles such as agendas, procedures, and decision-making processes.

* A team is interdependent; everyone works for the good of the team, not for oneself.

* Effective teams distinguish task from process. How they do things (the process) is just as important, if not more important, than what they do (the task).

Self-Directed Teams

A self-directed team is a team that is responsible for a whole product or process. The team plans the work and performs it, managing many of the tasks supervision or management might have done in the past. A facilitator (selected by the team or an outside individual) helps the group get started and stay on track. The facilitator's role decreases as the team increases its ability to work together effectively.

E-Teams

An e-team is a group of individuals who work across space and organizational boundaries with links strengthened by webs of communication technology. Members have complementary skills and are committed to a common purpose, have interdependent performance goals, and share an approach to work for which they hold themselves mutually accountable.

Geographically dispersed teams allow organizations to hire and retain the best people regardless of location. An e-team does not always imply telecommuters, individuals who work from home. Many virtual teams in today's organizations consist of employees both working at home and in small groups in the office, but in different geographic locations.

The benefits of an e-team approach are:

- Workers can be located anywhere in the world

- Virtual environments can give shy participants a new voice

- Members have less commuting and travel time, so they tend to be more productive

- Companies gain an increasingly horizontal organization structure, characterized by structurally, and geographically distributed human resources.

There are a few caveats when using e-teams. They frequently operate from multiple time zones, so it is important to make sure that there is some overlapping work time. In addition, unless a camera is used for meetings, working virtually means that there is no face to face body language to enhance communications. Therefore, intra-team communications must be more formal than with a team whose members meet physically. Care also needs to be taken to make sure no one is left out of the communications loop just because he or she is not visible. E-teams demand a high trust culture.

Chapter 3 – The First Stage of Team Development – Forming

What makes up a good team? Well, that question is open to interpretation, but we will start with the first step in the team building process which is forming. We will discuss what makes up that stage and how each person in the team fits into the process.

Hallmarks of This Stage

When a new team forms, it concerns itself with becoming oriented. It does this through testing. It tests to discover the boundaries of interpersonal and task behavior. At the same time, the members are establishing dependency relationships with leaders, fellow team members, or any standards that existed when the group formed. The behaviors of orientation, testing, and dependence become the process called Forming.

Members behave independently when the team forms. While there may be good will towards fellow members, unconditional trust is not yet possible.

Work during the Forming stage is categorized as follows:

Tasks	Processes that occur
Introductions	Uncertainty
Coming together	Apprehension
First agenda	Excitement

What to Do As a Leader

Strong leadership skills are essential in the Forming stage. The leader must:

- Provide an environment for introductions

- Create a climate where participants can begin to build rapport

- Present a solid first agenda so that the goals for the team are clear.

What to Do As a Follower

Because the members of a new team may experience uncertainty and apprehension, it's important to help members feel comfortable and that they are a part of the group. In addition, helping team members enhance their listening skills will allow them to focus more clearly on the objectives, thereby helping to maintain interest and enthusiasm for the work of the team.

Chapter 4 – The Second Stage of Team Development – Storming

We will look at the Storming phase where the team focuses on their objective. This is the reason the team was created, and we will break down where the leaders and followers fit into this stage. Team members will now begin to fill certain rolls and the team is starting to come together.

The Hallmarks of This Stage

In the Storming phase, the team starts to address the objective(s), suggesting ideas. It empowers itself to share leadership. Different ideas may compete for consideration, and if badly managed, this phase can be very destructive for the team. Egos emerge and turf wars occur. In extreme cases, the team can become stuck in this phase.

If a team is too focused on consensus, they may decide on a plan which is less effective to complete the task for the sake of the team. This carries its own set of challenges. It is essential that a team has strong facilitative leadership during this phase.

What to Do As a Leader

Team conflict is normal in this phase, and is a catalyst for creativity. But the leader must address any conflict immediately and directly so issues don't fester. Once you understand two sides to an issue, you can help the team generate a win-win solution. Assertive communication is an important skill during this phase of the group's evolution. It is also important to help team members continue to build trust.

What to Do As a Follower

A mind map is a diagram used to represent words, ideas, tasks, or other items linked to and arranged around a central key word or idea. Mind maps are used to generate, visualize, structure, and classify ideas, and as an aid in study, organization, problem solving, decision making, and writing.

The elements of a given mind map are arranged intuitively according to the importance of the concepts, and are classified into groupings, branches, or areas, with the goal of representing semantic or other connections between portions of information.

By presenting ideas in a radial, graphical, non-linear manner, mind maps encourage a brainstorming approach to planning and organizational tasks.

Chapter 5 – The Third Stage of Team Development – Norming

By now the team should be in place and everyone has their role with progress beginning on the objectives. Goals have been set and people are now beginning to work on their tasks.

The Hallmarks of This Stage

As the team moves out of the Storming phase, it enters the Norming phase. This tends to be a move towards harmonious working practices. Teams begin agreeing on the rules and values by which they operate. In the ideal situation, teams begin to trust themselves during this phase as they accept the vital contributions of each member toward achieving the team's goals.

What to Do As a Leader

As individual members take greater responsibility, team leaders can take a step back from the leadership role at this stage. It is an opportune time to provide team members with task and process tools, or even an energizer to keep enthusiasm levels high.

What to Do As a Follower

Because team members have gained some mutual trust, they are freer to focus on process and task. Being a link in a chain is a great way to visualize followers in this stage. If one link is not pulling its weight, or is not as strong as the other links the chance of success is lessened. Everyone needs to work together.

Chapter 6 – The Fourth Stage of Team Development – Performing

The team should now be well into their work and progress made on their objectives. Communication is going well and team members are sharing knowledge and working well together.

Hallmarks of this Stage

Once teams move from Norming to Performing, they are identified by high levels of independence, motivation, knowledge, and competence. Decision making is collaborative and dissent is expected and encouraged as there will be a high level of respect in the communication between team members.

What to Do As a Leader

Since the team is functioning in a highly independent way in the Performing phase, the leader shifts partially into a support and mentoring role to provide task or process resources to help the team complete its objectives.

What to Do As a Follower

Because the Performing stage implies high interpersonal trust, knowledge, and competence, participants can perform higher level analyses to support decisions toward team objectives.

A SWOT analysis (Strengths, Weaknesses, Opportunities, and Threats) is a simple tool that allows specific ideas to be easily categorized to help support the adoption of a solution to an objective.

Chapter 7 – Team Building Activities

Team building is an organized effort to improve team effectiveness. All members of the team must be committed to the idea in order for the effort to be effective. Team building can be indicated for any team or for a work team that is considered to be" in trouble". Team building implies hard work that continues on after the initial training session.

The Benefits and Disadvantages

The Benefits:

- Team building improves productivity and motivation.

- Teams will gain and increase ability to solve problems.

- Team building helps break down personal and political barriers and allows for rapport building.

- The process can help level the playing field between outgoing and shy team members.

- Participating in team building can help teams overcome performance problems.

The Disadvantages:

- Team building requires expert facilitation in order to be successful. Not every team leader has innate facilitation skills.

- Activities can be time-consuming for teams with a short-term charter. And if team members are part-time, they may have conflicting feelings about the time the team building takes.

- If several levels of management are on the team, those members may be reluctant to open up.

- Conducting team building activities electronically or by conference cannot be as effective face-to-face sessions.

- Some team building exercises involve touching or physical movement, which can make some people uncomfortable.

Team-Building Activities That Won't Make People Cringe

There are many choices of activities and techniques to foster team building. Which you choose depends upon your assessment of the team, the skill sets of the members, the amount of available time, geographical considerations or constraints, and the team's objectives.

Choosing a Location for Team-Building

A team building session can be intense, and often involves games or other physical exercises. It's important, therefore to select the location carefully to promote the best possible learning outcome. Regardless of whether you hold your team building session on or off site, there are some important considerations to explore.

Chapter 8 – Making the Most of Team Meetings

They are extremely important in team building and facilitation. It is very important that they are well structured and have a set purpose and time. When a meeting is run well it is a fantastic tool as it provides a forum where a lot of information can be given to a lot of people in a short amount of time. Issues can be addressed and action plans set into play.

Setting the Time and the Place

Giving thought to time and place considerations for a team meeting can go a long way toward producing a more effective meeting outcome. Below are some elements to think about.

- Is the location convenient for participants?

- Quiet. Is the meeting going to be held in an open environment? Near the plant?

- Is this an e-team meeting? Or a meeting with members in remote locations or different time zones?

- What time of day is best?

- Are there time zone considerations for e-teams or remote participants?

- For what other interruptions and distractions can you anticipate and plan?

Trying the 50-Minute Meeting

In some companies, meetings are stacked up on the hour like planes in the landing pattern at O'Hare Airport. The 50-minute meeting concept is simple; instead of a full 60-minute meeting, why not give people time for a bio break, a fresh cup of coffee, and "commuting time" to the next meeting?

50-minute meetings also help manage:

- Overload of information that the mind can absorb at one time

- Wandering attention spans

- Potential health problems from sitting too long

You can't always have a 50 minute meeting, but if you're meeting will run several hours, you could have a connected series of 50 minute meetings. The extra 10 minutes in each hour -- set at a consistent clock time such as 50 minutes after the hour -- could allow for stretches, breaks, or a quick e-mail session.

Using Celebrations of All Sizes

The team just finished a ten-month project to implement SAP in a small manufacturing company. The project delivered on time, and under budget. It's time to celebrate! Celebrations can take many forms. A checklist of elements to consider can help you decide how best to say thanks.

Chapter 9 – Solving Problems as a Team

One of the most common objectives of a team is to solve a certain problem. It is usually why a team is created. Team members bring a diverse set of skills to the team and this provides a great scenario and the best chance in finding a solution. Because the team is comprised of individuals that bring a unique skill set, it provides the team with a "the whole is greater than its parts" setup which is a valuable tool.

The Six Thinking Hats

In 1999, Dr. Edward de Bono published a book entitled <u>Six Thinking Hats</u>. He theorizes that the human brain thinks in a number of distinct ways -- or states -- which can be identified, deliberately accessed, and therefore planned for use in a structured way, allowing team members to develop strategies for thinking about particular issues.

Six Thinking Hats is a powerful technique that helps teams look at important decisions from a number of different perspectives. It helps them make better decisions by pushing members to move outside their habitual ways of thinking. It helps them understand the full complexity of a decision, and identify issues and opportunities which they might not otherwise notice.

In order to make it easier to clearly identify and work with these states, colored hats are used as metaphors for them. The act of putting on a colored hat allows individuals to symbolically think in terms of the state, either actually or imaginatively.

White Hat: Neutrality: Participants make statements of fact, including identifying information that is absent -- and presenting the views of people who are not present -- in a factual manner. Examples of this the results of this thinking are:

Red Hat: Feeling: Participants state their feelings, exercising their gut instincts. In many cases this is a method for harvesting ideas; it is not a question of recording statements, but rather getting everyone to identify their top two or three choices from a list of ideas or items identified under another hat. This is done to help reducing lists of many options into a few to focus on by allowing each participant to vote for the ones they prefer. It is applied more quickly than the other hats to ensure it is a gut reaction feeling that is recorded. This method can use post-it notes to allow a quick system of voting, and creates a clear visual cue that creates rapid if incomplete agreement around an issue.

Alternatively it may be used to state ones gut reaction or feelings on an issue under discussion - this is more common when using the hats to review personal progress or deal with issues where there is high emotional content that is relevant to discussion. Finally, this hat can be used to request an aesthetic response to a particular design or object.

Black Hat: Negative Judgment: Participants identify barriers, hazards, risks, and other negative connotations. This is critical thinking, looking for problems and mismatches. This hat is usually natural for people to use, the issues with it are that people will tend to use it when it is not requested and when it is not appropriate, thus stopping the flow of others. Preventing inappropriate use of the black hat is a common obstacle and vital step to effective group thinking. Another difficulty faced is that some people will naturally start to look for the solutions to raised problems - they start practicing green on black thinking before it is requested.

Yellow hat – Positive Judgment: Participants identify benefits associated with an idea or issue. This is the opposite of black hat thinking and looks for the reasons in favor of something. This is still a matter of judgment; it is an analytical process, not just blind optimism. One is looking to create justified statements in favor. It is encapsulated in the idea of "undecided positive" (whereas the black hat would be skeptical - undecided negative). The outputs may be statements of the benefits that could be created with a given idea, or positive statements about the likelihood of achieving it or identifying the key supports available that will benefit this course of action

Green Hat: Creative Thinking: This is the hat of thinking new thoughts. It is based around the idea of provocation and thinking for the sake of identifying new possibilities. Things are said for the sake of seeing what they might mean, rather than to form a judgment. This is often carried out on black hat statements in order to identify how to get past the barriers or failings identified there (green on black thinking). Because green hat thinking covers the full spectrum of creativity, it can take many forms.

Blue Hat: The Big Picture: This is the hat under which all participants discuss the thinking process. The facilitator will generally wear it throughout and each member of the team will put it on from time to time to think about directing their work together. This hat should be used at the start and end of each thinking session, to set objectives, to define the route to take to get to them, to evaluate where the group has got to, and where the thinking process is going. Having a facilitator maintain this role throughout helps ensure that the group remains focused on task and improves their chances of achieving their objectives.

Encouraging Brainstorming

Brainstorms are a simple and effective method for generating ideas and suggestions. They allow group members to use each other as creative resources and are effective when a subject is being introduced. The goal is to rapidly generate a large quantity of ideas. Subsequent sorting and prioritizing of the ideas is usually needed to refine the results.

Building Consensus

Consensus is a point of maximum agreement so action can follow. It is a win-win situation in which everyone feels that he or she has one solution that does not compromise any strong convictions or needs. To reach consensus, group members share ideas, discuss, evaluate, organize, and prioritize ideas, and struggle to reach the best conclusions together.

A good test for consensus is to ask the question "can you support this decision?" If everyone can support it, the group has achieved 100% consensus.

Consensus is not always the best strategy. In some cases, reaching consensus does not result in a better decision or outcome. For example, group members are capable of unanimously agreeing on a completely incorrect solution to a problem. But generally, reaching consensus remains a highly desirable goal.

To make consensus work, the leader must become skilled at separating the content of the team's work (the task) from the process (how the team goes about doing the task). But the process should get the most attention. A facilitative leader helps a team to solve its own problem. The problem-solving process is as follows:

1. Identify the problem or goal.

2. Generate alternative solutions.

3. Establish objective criteria.

4. Decide on a solution that best fits the criteria.

5. Proceed with the solution.

6. Evaluate the solution.

Everyone involved in the process should understand exactly which step is being worked on at any given point. When team members sense a problem, they are usually reacting to symptoms of the problem. But they are side effects of the real problem which usually lies below the surface.

Chapter 10 – Encouraging Teamwork

For every team member that believes and works for the team the chances of success go up exponentially. That is the reason why it is so important in teamwork and team building, as it provides the greats chance of success.

Some Things to Do

- Promote an active learning climate for the team

- Try to relate the team building strategies to the team's work

- Don't be afraid to experiment with new strategies

- Constantly evaluate both your output and your process. In short, ask regularly, *"How are we doing?"*

Some Things to Avoid

- Being aggressive -- instead of assertive

- Failing to let others express their opinions

- Inadequate planning

Some Things to Consider

Encouraging teamwork means making a commitment, and requires practice. The process is not instant and take some time, so be patient. Do not be discouraged by mistakes, learn from them.

The 90 Minute Guide series of books covers a variety of general business skills and are intended to be completed in 90 minutes or less. It is an effective way for building your skill set and can be used to acquire professional development units needed by project managers and other industries to maintain their certification. For the availability of titles please see

https://www.silvercitypublications.com/shop/.

No. 1 - Appreciative Inquiry

No. 2 - Assertiveness and Self Control

No. 3 - Attention Management

No. 4 - Body Language Basics

No. 5 - Business Acumen

No. 6 - Business and Etiquette

No. 7 - Change Management

No. 8 - Coaching and Mentoring

No. 9 - Communications Strategies

No. 10 - Conflict Resolution

No. 11 - Creative Problem Solving

No. 12 - Delivering Constructive Criticism

No. 13 - Developing Creativity

No. 14 - Developing Emotional Intelligence

No. 15 - Developing Interpersonal Skills

No. 16 - Developing Social Intelligence

No. 17 - Employee Motivation

No. 18 - Facilitation Skills

No. 19 - Goal Setting and Getting Things Done

No. 20 - Knowledge Management Fundamentals

No. 21 - Leadership and Influence

No. 22 - Lean Process and Six Sigma Basics

No. 23 - Managing Anger

No. 24 - Meeting Management

No. 25 - Negotiation Skills

No. 26 - Networking Inside a Company

No. 27 - Networking Outside a Company

No. 28 - Office Politics for Managers

No. 29 - Organizational Skills

No. 30 - Performance Management

No. 31 - Presentation Skills

No. 32 - Public Speaking

No. 33 - Servant Leadership